I Love Meetings

I Love Meetings:

7 Rules for Effective Meetings

Nava Laguerre

No part of this publication may be reproduced, distributed, or transmitted in any form or by any means, including photocopying, recording, or other electronic or mechanical methods, or by any information storage and retrieval system without the prior written permission of the author, except in the case of very brief quotations embodied in critical reviews and certain other noncommercial uses permitted by copyright law.

Copyright ©2021 by Nava Laguerre. All rights reserved

Dedicated to my family, with love.

Table of Contents

Introduction	1
Why I Wrote This Book	1
Meetings: Love Them or Hate Them?	2
Chapter 1	5
Set the Tone	5
Purpose	6
Focus	9
Mood	13
Personal Tone	14
Body Language	15
Verbal Contributions	18
Conclusion	20
Chapter 2	21
Respect the Time	21
Start with the Agenda	22
Meet with Purpose	23
Use Meeting Time Efficiently	25
Deliberate Small Talk	29
Conclusion	31

Chapter 3 — 33

Speakers' Perceptions — 33
- Where Do You Fit into the Equation? — 33
- Be a Plus as a Speaker — 34
- Conclusion — 38

Chapter 4 — 41

Invite the Right People — 41
- What's the Meeting Costing You? — 42
- Include the Right People — 43
- Conclusion — 46

Chapter 5 — 49

Have Fewer Meetings — 49
- Add Meetings (But of Different Types) — 50
- And Then Subtract — 51
- Use Collaboration Tools — 52
- Conclusion — 53

Chapter 6 — 55

Close the Loop — 55
- Gain Traction (Don't Spin Your Wheels) — 55
- Conclusion — 57

Chapter 7	59
Build on the Overall Goal	59
Set the Tone Again	59
Decide Who Carries the Ball	61
Conclusion	62
Afterword	65
Acknowledgments	67
About the Author	69
References	71

Introduction

Why I Wrote This Book

I developed a real passion for well-executed meetings from participating in my fair share of meetings: some great, some good, and enough of them which could be improved. It is because of the latter that I decided to write this book, highlighting the ways that meetings can become more efficient and productive.

After sitting through enough meetings, I started to think deeply about how meetings should be conducted as if an expert were performing an art. In my experience, some meetings weren't run at an expert level at all. Some moderators performed like a top athlete demonstrating their craft, others, like second-rate performers. Many meetings however, were, as Leslie Perlow puts it, "(1) too frequent, (2) poorly timed, and (3) badly run, leading to losses in productivity, collaboration, and well-being for both groups and individuals."[1]

Another reason these meetings left me unimpressed is because management tolerates others who think just because they're not in senior positions, they have less accountability and therefore it's acceptable to under-prepare for meetings or presentations.

As a junior associate sitting in enough meetings moderated by those who were in senior roles and yet gave subpar performances in terms of how

Introduction

they let these meetings play out, I wanted to write a book to talk about how such meetings are viewed from our perspective and provide some tips.

Aside from personal experience, I reached out to a few trusted individuals to crowdsource some illustrations. The examples listed are either mine or shared by others who granted me permission to retell them. Although I do not have senior executive level experience, it is my hope that you will find some of these scenarios useful and even be inspired by a few to implement changes in your meetings.

Meetings: Love Them or Hate Them?

Everyone hates meetings, right? Well, that's not necessarily true. Some of us enjoy and look forward to the professional exchange of ideas and the development of meaningful action plans as well as the social interaction that takes place before and after meetings. There is, however, a general perception in organizations everywhere that people hate meetings...or at least that we should.

If most employees don't hate meetings, why do so many people claim that they do? Maybe it's because a lot of people are vocal about seeing meetings as a waste of time, as distractions from their "real" work and as disruptions to their work day. Given these sentiments, it's easy to jump on the "I hate meetings" bandwagon.

Many people do dread meetings though, and for good reason. Meetings can and should be fruitful, but all too often, they are not as effective and useful as they could be. Time is wasted, meeting goals and action plans are not clearly defined or followed, and attendees leave the meeting confused or frustrated with the feeling that nothing was accomplished. I read in a Forbes article,

> employees who attend more meetings throughout the day feel more tired and rushed to complete their other job responsibilities. How employees feel about meetings — often negatively, further influences their job satisfaction and perceptions of the organization overall.[2]

Ultimately, there are few jobs that will not require employees to attend meetings and few workplaces that do not hold regular meetings for their staff.

This short book presents seven themes to keep in mind when planning and conducting meetings. There are tips, stories, and examples in each of these themes, intended to help you and your colleagues make the most of meeting time and empower you to cancel or shorten meetings that are unnecessary or too long.

Whether you moderate or mainly participate, I hope that part of this book will resonate. As you plan for your next meeting, whether virtual or in person, may the guidelines in these chapters allow

Introduction

you to streamline your meetings, making them more productive, gratifying, and useful for your employees and your corporation.

Chapter 1

Set the Tone

Tone is the foundation of everything in this book. From the planning stage to the end of the actual meeting, establishing and maintaining the proper tone throughout ensures that every other aspect of the meeting will generally fall into place. This means that time and opinions are respected, information is clear, and goals to be accomplished outside of the meetings are agreed to, all of which results in effective, respectful, useful, and productive meetings. Conversely, without the proper foundation, attendees will walk away feeling that their voices, time, and work have not been respected. When the proper tone is set and the direction of the meeting is clear and positive, attendees will leave the meeting with a sense of collaboration, clarity, usefulness, productivity, and motivation.

Setting the tone for the meeting covers more than just whether the meeting is interesting or arid. It is about purpose, focus, and mood.

Chapter 1

Purpose

How many times have you heard a colleague say, or even said yourself, "Why are we having this meeting?" Every meeting must have a clear purpose that is understood by all who attend. I'll talk more about respecting people's time in Chapter 2, but part of that respect is the establishment for everyone that the meeting has purpose that is relevant to them. If the meeting has no purpose or if the purpose isn't clear, people will feel that their time is wasted.

Harvard Business Review reports that when they surveyed 182 senior managers in a range of industries,

> 65% of them felt that meetings kept them from completing their own work; 71% said meetings were unproductive and inefficient; 64% said meetings often come at the expense of deep thinking; and 62% said meetings miss opportunities to bring the team closer together.[1]

Needless to say, these are not good numbers! So what's missing for these respondents? A clear sense of purpose.

MeetingSift outlines six main types of meetings, each with their own purpose:

1. **Status Update Meetings:** Attendees take stock of how the project is progressing and talk about next steps.

2. **Information-Sharing Meetings:** Moderators dispense information. Attendees are often passive except to seek further information or clarification.

3. **Decision-Making Meetings:** Participants discuss and then reach consensus on issues and action plans.

4. **Problem-Solving Meetings:** Attendees strategize and plan out an approach to rectify a problem by drawing up and agreeing upon an action plan.

5. **Innovation Meetings:** Team members collectively evaluate and discuss innovative proposals. They make recommendations for and ultimately agree upon action plans.

6. **Team-Building Meetings:** These meetings serve to create and strengthen team relationships, motivate team members towards a common goal, enhance corporate culture, and embolden team members. [2]

Finally, I'd like to add a seventh type of "meeting" to this list. This is generally not considered a meeting at all, but nevertheless, I propose treating that "morning check-in" with a colleague or employee and that "quick call to verify or clarify something" as a meeting by keeping them precise — as they are meant to be. Just as we should have structured, formal meetings, may those moments to quickly touch base have some element of efficiency as well.

> 7. **Check-in and Detail-Gathering Meetings:** Colleagues briefly check in and greet each other to touch base, exchange updates, and seek or provide answers to quick questions.

I once worked at an organization where the "morning check-in" often turned into an hour-long conversation. Some people truly don't get the concept of small talk, be it in person or remote, likewise the notion of making a quick call to confirm something. Instead, they trap others into long-winded discussions with no regard for how they are impacting another's time, schedule, or workload. While it's nice to make small talk, and doing so is part of relationship building, both participants don't necessarily have that much time to allocate to a quick call or morning greeting, and the person who carried on with a long dialogue has just impinged on the other's time, possibly curtailing their work plan and schedule for that day. Because not everyone has the same toolkit for managing chitchat and social interaction, it's important to at least have a sense that even "casual" interactions have some element of order when conducted in the workplace. Reserve idle chitchat for lunch or coffee breaks.

For companies with offices around the world, and with many people working from home, these firms have been thrown into a tizzy trying to help everyone feel and stay connected. The tendency has been to hold virtual, companywide gatherings. However, it is understandable that a video conference with the entire office may not feel intimate and each department could wish to meet separately. I suggest scheduling time to briefly and informally catch up and check in with team members or colleagues one-on-one or in small groups to see each other's faces. This is also a good panacea for those who may not be comfortable showing their faces in web meetings with hundreds of attendees.

Focus

In order for a meeting to be productive, it has to have focus. Part of focus is ensuring that time is used effectively (more about this in Chapter 2), which includes making sure the meeting stays on track.

As the moderator, ensure the purpose of the meeting is clear in advance so that attendees arrive prepared and knowing what to expect. Stick to that purpose throughout the meeting. It's easy for speakers to go off topic, and when that happens, the entire meeting can easily veer off course, resulting in a deviation from its purpose and a loss of focus.

For example, as soon as a Key Performance Indicator (KPI) meeting becomes an IT issues-themed discussion, then it has derailed and the focus has been lost. The meeting is in danger of

Chapter 1

not achieving its objective and the moderator needs to get it back to its focal point.

I once had a colleague who repeatedly complained about the low salary during each meeting, and those in management consistently took time out of the Sales KPI meeting to actually discuss it rather than nip it in the bud. Another colleague would often opine over IT issues at each KPI meeting. At first, I'd be in consternation, wondering how these colleagues failed to realize that which was evident to the rest of us. Eventually, it dawned on me that not everyone possesses a natural sense of how to conduct oneself in corporate settings. This awareness is not rudimentary to all, which I believe was the case for both individuals. I'm convinced it would be advantageous for some people to undergo training in how to perform in meetings. It's not that these colleagues stepped out of bounds, but rather, that they exhibited a lack of cognizance for corporate-type meeting standards. They missed salient and basic cues in terms of how to behave in such gatherings. If you think about it, meetings are performances in themselves. Once you fall too much out of the role/character, the audience (i.e., other participants) is disrupted.

No, we can't expect managers to become sociologists; this is why I highly recommend putting personnel through basic "socially acceptable meeting behaviors," (i.e., training which expands beyond the general *isms* topics.) Those of us with this perception should set an example by being patient and gracious, and we should help elevate others to the degree expected of them. However, once an employee has gone through the "socially acceptable meeting behaviors," training yet carries on with an unchanged attitude, even after receiving honest feedback (which I'd interpret as not living up to expectations), at that point, the behavior is *malsain*[3] to the team.

In the above examples, a KPI meeting was not the appropriate setting for discussing salary issues. Nor should a KPI meeting become an IT issues dialogue. Rather, the moderator should request the attendee consult with the right department and, if necessary, arrange for the team to meet at a later time on these tangential issues. However, the moderator should be sentient to how recurring IT issues reasonably impact the team's ability to be productive. If the same unrelated issues emerge at specific meetings, it is a clear indication of a need for a different type of meeting.

How many of us have worked with that one person who just won't stop talking and making irrelevant comments? These people are everywhere — at every company — always wanting to talk, and waste other people's time. Some people do love the sound of their own voice, and yes, they make pertinent contributions; however, they can go on too long and perhaps give the wrong impression that they just want to talk for the sake of being the center of attention. I often think about the cost of their garrulity to the company. Time is money, and any time your organization spends on unnecessary activity diminishes the bottom line.

Recently, I was speaking with a former instructor who raised that same point. If only companies considered the cost of meetings, I believe there would be fewer meetings and, at the very least, some people would be invited to fewer of them because there isn't much value added to their presence at some meetings. A suggestion I learned from a Lynda.com course (Lynda.com is now LinkedIn Learning) some years ago, is for moderators to quickly and decisively deal with the non-stop talker: set the tone with a reminder that most of the meeting will follow more of a "listen and take note" format. Attendees will be called upon at an opportune time to comment, seek clarification, and/or ask questions. By announcing this, the moderator signals to everyone that comments that are off topic are not welcome.

Now to address moderators directly. Frankly put, moderators do themselves and their teams a favor by keeping meetings on course. In fact, it's their job! Whenever new or unrelated issues are brought up, it is reasonable to swiftly hit the brakes and propose another meeting to discuss these other issues.

I will now personally entreat you, the moderator who is sometimes hesitant to crack the whip, and you, yes, you the attendee with the habit of going off on tangents, please stay focused. Please, please, please stop making the rest of us participate in futile meetings! Stick to the meeting topic at hand, schedule different meetings for divergent issues, and in those meetings, kindly invite only the people who are impacted or involved. To everyone else, who is perfect, thank you!

Mood

Just as you don't want to be the one who carries on with irrelevant remarks and distractions, don't be the negative contributor. When you set up a meeting to discuss specific problems that need to be addressed, be part of the solution rather than merely bringing forth issues and leaving them for others to solve.

I've been in meetings to discuss persistent tech issues yet found the moderator spent one-third of the time debating a well-established obstacle rather than focusing on its resolution. I feel compelled to remind people that no IT system is flawless; even the best system will not function to your exact preference, nor should it — it was not tailor-made for you. Instead of nagging, one way you can add value as an employee is to develop work-arounds that can be used by others in your company. To endlessly complain about issues without offering solutions plainly labels you as **The Complainer**, and each instance you complain, the rest of us increasingly view you as living up to your label. Be part of the solution.

I have worked at a few places where some colleagues were known as those who only raised their hands to lament. When a moderator asks if there are any questions, it is not an invitation to nitpick but a call to pose meaningful, relevant questions. (There is no such thing as a "silly question" if someone genuinely needs clarification on a point, but there is a big difference between seemingly "silly" questions asked out of earnest when seeking information versus questions or comments raised mainly to argue, gripe, or be vocal.)

There are those who always have an issue — a problem to kvetch about — and that kind of energy/behavior is draining to the rest of us in attendance. As a friend of mine puts it, it's disruptive, not constructive. It is always more welcoming to state your input in a straightforward and beneficial manner.

Personal Tone

It is also important to mind your tone so as not to come across as too emphatic. I was made aware that I speak rather emphatically about everything, often making people think I have a peremptory, or worse, imperious tone. In hindsight, I recognize that my inclination to speak in this way may have prevented others from sharing their feedback for fear of appearing confrontational. If you have a valid contribution to the discussion, make your point without being either apologetic or condescending. There is a fine line between resolute and insolent.

Some people naturally and unintentionally come across as intimidating or contrite, and so you may need to analyze and adjust your personality in order to come across more professionally and less (or more) forcefully. Also, don't be afraid to hold your ground in debates or discussions where multiple perspectives need to be considered, but avoid being patronizing or overly assertive. Every perspective is valid, and if an agreement needs to be reached, the best solution will ultimately come to the surface, so argue your points politely and professionally.

Overall, when it comes to personal tone, your aim is to always be self-assured, respectful and approachable.

Body Language

It is said that 70-80% of communication is non-verbal. In meetings, you should therefore consider not just your words but also your body language. Your body language needs to show interest, attentiveness, and openness. Have you ever watched a video of yourself and been surprised by what you saw? Your body language may be saying something you are not aware of.

Be attentive to these aspects of your body language:

> **Eye contact:** Making and maintaining eye contact in North American culture shows that you are mindful and interested in what the other person is saying. But don't stare. If the presenter is showing slides or a video, alternate your gaze between their media and them. Looking at your cell phone, at other participants, or

around the room will give the message that you are indifferent or distracted.

If you have colleagues who come from other cultures (I hope you do!), be aware that for some, making and maintaining direct eye contact may be interpreted as a form of aggression or an attempt to intimidate. As the speaker, if you notice someone isn't making eye contact with you, consider whether it might simply be a cultural difference. If so, don't take it personally.

Sitting posture: Sit up straight in your chair, maintain good posture, and even lean forward a little when someone is speaking. Leaning towards them shows you are "leaning into" what they are saying; this shows your receptiveness to their message. Don't cross your arms, as this can be interpreted as a sign that you are closing yourself off to what the speaker or presenter is saying. And don't slouch. Slouching indicates that you are apathetic, bored, or feeling defeated or discouraged. It also suggests a lack of confidence. Similarly, leaning back in your chair too casually may indicate that you aren't taking the meeting seriously. Even if you are not enjoying the meeting, err on the safe side and maintain a professional presence.

Like the warning labels on the packages of silica in the new shoes you just bought that say "Do

Not Eat," some things are so obvious that they shouldn't need to be said but I'm going to say it anyway — pay attention in the meeting! Even if you don't feel the meeting is a good use of your time, you've been asked to attend, and so remain professional and attentive. Don't surf the internet on your laptop, doodle, use your cell phone, or chat with the person beside you.

Here's an extreme example, but it happened. An acquaintance of mine once attended a meeting where her direct supervisor fell asleep while someone else was presenting. He and the laptop which had been sitting on his lap went crashing to the ground, causing everyone to turn around, first in horror. Later on everyone bursted out laughing. It was a pretty informal meeting and the attendees all knew each other well, so even though he was embarrassed, his humiliation was the worst that happened (fortunately, the laptop escaped unscathed). But in a more formal meeting with prominent stakeholders, falling asleep and crashing to the ground with your laptop could be a deal breaker and isn't going to help your career prospects!

Remember that it is quite evident to others in the meeting if you aren't paying attention. When you are the one presenting, you will expect the attention of others, so the least you can do is give them yours and be the audience member you would want to have during your presentation.

Chapter 1

Verbal Contributions

Be respectful, but also command respect.

At one corporation where I worked, the team would often talk loudly over the young female manager while she was presenting. However, whenever this happened, she was not shy about taking control and reminding those disturbing the meeting that she was talking and therefore expected them to pay attention. The guys on the team were shocked the first few times she took charge and afterwards talked about her authoritative demeanor and intolerance. But you know what? They eventually exhibited the utmost reverence for her. Although they were uncomfortable being chastised in front of their fellow colleagues, they in fact admired her ability to voice herself and command respect. This was a seminal moment for me and served as inspiration to find my own voice and not shy away from expressing it.

As an added bonus, that same manager never used the word "mistake." Instead, she talked about "opportunity for improvement." Who wouldn't welcome an opportunity to improve? Her temperament, careful choice of words, and her expectation of respect were truly great traits of hers that I admired.

In a less inspiring situation, I had two critical, tension-filled encounters. In one meeting, I once had a senior manager who shook hands with others but offered me, the only Black person in the room, a fist bump, along with the comment, "Fist bump, like Michelle and Barack." Another time, that same person turned to me and said, "Ya know what I'm sayin'?" whereas to others, he would say, "...if that makes sense?" I was told, once while giving advice on how to guest-host his program, Johnny Carson advised Gore Vidal (this isn't a joke): if you're unsure about a joke don't say it! To sum it up, please discreetly consider any jokes you may be tempted to make. Think carefully before making them; humor is neither universal, nor is it always appropriate.

Don't bad-mouth your colleagues. In one of my workplaces, I was the newest member of the small *equipe*[4] where at nearly every meeting, most of them would rail against personnel from other departments. This behavior made me so uncomfortable and raised doubts in my mind as to whether their actions were the same in my absence. Personal feelings aside, badmouthing colleagues is simply tactless.

Don't discriminate. I often wonder if management, or anyone really, is conscious that their preferences can be revealed through the level of excitement they express towards a certain person compared to others. I have seen the reactions to presentations vary from "Ok, thanks" for one presenter to "Great! Perfect! Excellent!" for another, although their respective presentations didn't seem to warrant the difference. If your favoritism is so blatant to others, then you may want to practice how to maintain an element of neutrality and be more mindful to treat people equally.

Conclusion

In a certain way, meetings can be deemed as performances; you are there to enact whatever role you play. Leadership is responsible for setting the tone, but it is also each attendee's duty to contribute to a positive, productive tone in meetings. Remain professional in your words and actions, and the foundation will be set for a high-yielding, useful meeting.

Chapter 2

Respect the Time

Two common complaints about meetings are that they run over time and that they include agenda items that could and should be shared in an email rather than presented in a meeting.

If the tone has previously been set for meetings, and hopefully also for the organization as a whole, then ideally employees will be reading and responding accordingly to their emails. If this is happening, then holding a meeting in order to simply present basic information is not necessary. Information meetings may be necessary when a large amount of complex details need to be presented and discussed, but if an email suffices, send it and forego the meeting.

When meetings are required, however, keep in mind that everyone has no shortage of work to do outside of the meeting time. They have scheduled their day with, for example, a one-hour meeting in mind, so respect the time parameters of the meeting and the flow of people's work days.

Chapter 2

Start with the Agenda

Start by drawing up a clear agenda. This should go without saying, but some meetings don't even have an agenda. An agenda is a must so that attendees know the purpose of the meeting and can plan for discussions or presentations, whether as a presenter or a listener. At the very least, "The agenda provides a compass for the conversation, so the meeting can get back on track if the discussion wanders off course."[1]

The agenda should be focused and have a natural flow, moving from topic to topic. Having a tight, focused agenda will allow you to keep to a schedule.

According to Indeed, Career Guide's "<u>How to Write an Agenda: Tips, Template and Sample</u>," following these steps will ensure your agenda is tight and clear:

1. Identify the meeting's goals.

2. Ask participants for input.

3. List the questions you want to address.

4. Identify the purpose of each task.

5. Estimate the amount of time to spend on each topic.

6. Identify who leads each topic.

7. End each meeting with a review. [2]

Distribute the agenda and any readings a few days prior to the meeting. Receiving agenda items some days in advance allows attendees time to review any materials that will be covered during the meeting. They can come prepared knowing the purpose and objectives of the meeting and ready to discuss and present their position on any decision items.

Moderators, ask ahead of time for agenda items others may wish or need to contribute so that you can prevent surprise, last-minute additions that will add time to the meeting. You will also likely want to review action items and allow for a question period at the end of the meeting or after specific agenda topics, so include those in the agenda as well.

Meet with Purpose

First and foremost, don't hold unnecessary meetings. If Tuesday at 10 am is the designated day and time for weekly staff meetings, don't meet just because it's Tuesday 10 am. If nothing needs follow-up, then cancel the meeting. Employees will be grateful for the time that is freed up so that they can attend to other work.

When a meeting is necessary, the moderator should ensure it starts on time. As the attendee, it's best to arrive a few minutes early to allow for chitchat and settling in.

Chapter 2

I am sure we've all been in meetings that started five or ten minutes late because one or more people hadn't arrived yet. While the late attendee might expect that others will wait so that they don't miss anything, it is, in fact, disrespectful for the moderator (and the person running late) to expect those who were on time to wait for the meeting to start, especially if a delay in beginning the meeting will result in it going over time. Start on time and don't use meeting time to fill in latecomers. It's their responsibility to catch up on what they missed. If someone is repeatedly late, they will soon learn that the meeting will start without them and they will (hopefully) start to arrive early. Don't be the person who always shows up late and then expects others to wait for you or to repeat what has already been covered.

If you are the moderator, run a tight ship! Whether the meeting is virtual or in person, stick to the agenda and keep the socializing to before or after the meeting. If your meeting is virtual, establish the expectation that the chat room in the online platform will be used for relevant comments or questions, not for small talk between attendees. Set aside a designated amount of time in the agenda for questions and discussion rather than taking questions during presentations. When presenters have no control and allow attendees to ask questions whenever they like, it leads to too many undue interruptions and disrupts the flow of the meeting — and the presenter's concentration.

Not to be redundant, but people, every meeting needs a clearly defined start and end time.

In "How to stop wasting your time—and everyone else's—in meetings," Terri Williams reports on a Clarizen/Harris Poll survey which "reveals that the average American worker spends 4.5 hours in general status meetings each week, and workers spend even longer (4.6 hours) just preparing for those meetings."[3] Out of a forty-hour work week, that's almost a quarter of someone's time, and so it's imperative to ensure that time is well spent. Look for ways to cut down on that number.

Use Meeting Time Efficiently

When you plan a meeting, assign the right people to suitable roles: chairing the meeting, timekeeping, taking minutes, operating the technology, etc.

Make sure that the person operating presentation tools during the meeting is adept at using them or survey other attendees beforehand to find the right person for the job. If there are technological issues during a media presentation, having the person operating the equipment fix the issue is the most efficient solution so that the presentation can continue as seamlessly as possible. If no one in the meeting is a tech expert, have one on speed dial in case any technical issues emerge and you need to solve them as quickly as possible. And, of course, whenever you are giving a video or any other presentation, prac-

Chapter 2

tice with the technology and review your presentation prior to the meeting to sort out any gaps or glitches. Not only is it embarrassing for you to be fighting with your laptop trying to get a video to start, but it also wastes people's time and derails the focus of the meeting.

Imagine that eight participants need to speak during the course of a sixty-minute meeting and there is a five-minute ice breaker/check-in, a three-minute rant from **BIG TALKER**, another three minutes allocated to **BIG COMPLAINER**, who also require five minutes to actually present their piece; then the moderator provides a status update for fifteen minutes, and another presenter needs to speak for five to seven minutes...so far only half of the participants have spoken, yet nearly 40 minutes have lapsed and four other attendees, each requiring about five minutes, haven't spoken, and there has to be time for questions/clarification. I'm exhausted (after writing that horrible run-on sentence! but also...) you'd be exhausted after listening to all the complaints and irrelevant conversations. At this point, your mind needs to get into information processing and discard mode, all the while remaining focused on the meeting's purpose. People's attention spans are not without limit. After an hour, regardless of how interesting or important the meeting may be, people will begin to tune out.

Setting the tone and respecting the time are tenets of preparation, discipline, and respect for oneself and attendees. Also, it might even make the meeting fruitful; *en passant*[4] it could even result in greater productivity.

In <u>an article published in Forbes</u>, writer Jamie Potter goes so far as to recommend that organizations

> have professional facilitators run meetings. This could be full-time employees hired on for just this purpose, external consultants, or even internal employees with other roles who are then trained and certified in meeting facilitation.[5]

He argues that professionally <u>trained facilitators</u> can improve on the efficiency and effectiveness of meetings. "Especially when the interests of various meeting attendees diverge, trained facilitators can ensure that <u>procedures are fairly followed</u> so that all walk away happy."[6]

Consider this: someone I've worked with attended a condo board meeting to discuss repair costs; note that owners were being asked to pay $5,000 each and made it clear they had questions. Rather than asking residents to submit their queries ahead of time, the board suggested residents raise their questions during the meeting. In consequence, the one-hour meeting became a three-hour-long spectacle where the board received a wave of ennui from over 100 residents. This is a clear case of when questions should have been requested ahead of time, and having a facilitator to ensure a "no-surprise outcome," as someone I know would say, would have been ideal. A facilitator would have served as a mediator and mitigated such a debacle.

Do you remember the four-and-a-half hours per week spent in status meetings mentioned above? That alone is much more than 10% of a forty-hour work week. Think that over! To that end, Potter recommends cutting meeting times in half.[7] Is it time to rethink creating your agenda so that you have a short, snappy meeting covering all that needs to be covered? (And of course, plan the time accordingly.) If you have an hour booked for a meeting but after drafting the agenda it is clear you will only need half an hour, adjust the meeting time accordingly.

Likewise, if you are working through the meeting and it becomes clear you will finish early, then finish early. Terri Williams cites Bonnie Hagemann, co-author of *Leading with Vision* and CEO of Executive Development Associates, who recommends that meetings end as soon as the agenda is complete rather than lingering and talking about unrelated topics just because the scheduled time hasn't been filled.[8]

Lastly, if you are speaking, whether it be in a formal meeting or a quick "drive-by" in someone's office, be concise and get to your point. I mentioned tone in Chapter 1, and another reason to set the tone and keep control of the meeting and of the attendees (especially the talkers) is to respect the time. I challenge you to see respecting the time (i.e., starting and ending meetings on time) as an exercise of discipline. It also demonstrates respect to all participants.

Deliberate Small Talk

I want to be clear — I'm not advocating eliminating small talk from the workplace entirely. Socializing with colleagues is an important part of the workplace culture for building trusting and positive relationships, and let's face it, no one can be on task 100% of the time without needing a mental break. Water cooler chats are not only enjoyable, they are essential! Just make sure they don't take over the work day or derail meetings.

Using time efficiently also applies to "casual" meetings. When a colleague calls to rapidly verify something or stops by to briefly say hello, I challenge you to be considerate and think of it as a one- to two-minute meeting. Trapping them into a twenty-minute (or more) dialogue is taking advantage of their willingness to listen. We are social beings and therefore need to chat, but I suggest scheduling "catching up time" with each other over lunch breaks or as after-hours get-togethers rather than during work hours.

Some people purposely come early to meetings so that they can grab a drink and/or a snack and chat with other attendees while settling in. Likewise, some meeting attendees linger a bit afterwards to chat whereas others leave immediately and head back to their desks. These approaches give people the option to engage in the small talk

Chapter 2

— or not — simply by choosing to be there or to opt out.

However, with people working from home and more meetings happening virtually, many of the occasions for small talk have been lost. Frisch and Green have proposed a novel remedy. In their Harvard Business Review article, "<u>Make Time for Small Talk in your Virtual Meetings</u>," the authors emphasize that with the opportunities for chitchat having largely disappeared in the move to virtual meetings, it is important to forge channels to build small talk back into the environment. Those few minutes before the meeting as people are grabbing coffee and muffins together don't exist in virtual meetings. Also, it seems awkward to linger in the virtual room after the meeting has ended, and if the moderator closes the room, you may not have the opportunity to do so.[9] We all need to gab, but we can be more intentional about it. Why not schedule it?

Frisch and Green specify structured ways to add small talk in the meeting by including it in the agenda and assigning a specific period of time for it. They recommend using an icebreaker or a check-in at the beginning of meetings — a quick, "How are you/what's new with you personally or professionally?" Q&A in which each attendee can speak for a minute to connect with one another less formally.

Another option would be to leave unstructured time at the end of the meeting for people to remain in the virtual meeting room and socialize before getting back to individual tasks.[10] However, participants not staying longer can go on with their own work. The moderator can leave the room open and specify a designated time period so it doesn't go on endlessly — maybe ten minutes? Having this opportunity at the end of the meeting gives attendees the choice to participate or not and also doesn't take away from the formal meeting time. As a gentle reminder to moderators, do not forget to pre-set the room to close once the designated time is over.

Conclusion

Small talk or "casual meetings" are a necessary part of the work place. But we should approach these interactions in a constructive manner to not distract from the actual meeting. Start and end on time, keep to the agenda, and designate separate time to address tangents and questions. Keeping the focus throughout the meeting by adhering to the agenda will ensure that attendees leave the meeting space feeling that the meeting was effective, useful and that their time was respected.

Chapter 3

Speakers' Perceptions

If you've been invited to a meeting, chances are the moderator sees value in having you there. Therefore, as an attendee you want to play a meaningful role in the meeting; you will want to add value.

Where Do You Fit into the Equation?

John C. Maxwell, author of <u>How Successful People Grow</u>, and a plethora of other books on personal and professional growth, encourages his readers to be a plus, not a minus, in all relationships — personal and professional. His main point is, you are a plus if you add value to your organization and to your relationships. If you have nothing to add but always only take, then you are a minus.[1] (For a quick run-down on what he means, watch this short video clip: <u>"Minute with Maxwell: Are You a Plus or a Minus?"</u> — John Maxwell Team.)

In his article, <u>"How to Run a More Effective Meeting,"</u> Adam Bryant specifies three ways that people can be either a plus or a minus in meetings:

- Some people showboat/dominate the conversation; others remain passive/silent.

- Some people offer ideas and solutions; others only criticize or complain.

- Some people lack confidence and are hesitant to make suggestions or offer ideas that are beyond the scope of their experience or standing in the organization.[2]

Your attendance at a meeting will be much more appreciated if you are a plus.

Be a Plus as a Speaker

Ideally, everyone in attendance will be a plus. If you are speaking or leading part of the meeting, it's imperative that you be a plus. Your presentation needs to be useful and engaging for your audience, and remember they're rooting for you.

When you are called upon to present, that is not the time to be lost or unprepared. Don't claim you were unaware you were presenting. Chances are that is not actually genuine, and if it is true and you were put on the spot, then that needs to be discussed with the moderator at a later date to ensure it doesn't happen again. If the agenda was distributed ahead of time and your name was on it, be ready for your moment. If you're not clear on what is expected of you for your spot on the agenda, seek guidance prior to the meeting so you can prepare.

Whether you are given one minute or one hundred to present, you need to prepare, and your preparation needs to include the anticipation for three to five questions that may come up. Have those answers ready.

Arriving at the meeting but then claiming you didn't understand what had to be done, and therefore you can neither answer basic questions nor present without ad-libbing is untenable. You should know this leaves an opening for others to observe you as unprofessional and can lead them to perceive you as a minor league candidate, not ready for prime time (i.e., not suitable for greater responsibilities). Management may not raise this lack of preparation with you — they may wish to avoid that uncomfortable talk — but they're thinking it and have simply habituated themselves to your tenth-rate output.

I entreat you to **stop reading the slides to us. Please!** The basic (oft forgotten) rule of presentations is this: use slides to showcase the main points of a presentation, not to present paragraphs and large clumps of information that people in the back of the room probably can't read anyway. A PowerPoint or any other type of presentation is meant to be visual, so use the technology to highlight the main points that you then discuss. When creating your slides, make them visually captivating and less wordy. **Show** the highlights of your presentation in point form, but **tell**, with your verbal explanations, what the central objectives are. Meetings are meant to inform, inspire, and equip in order to bring about desired outcomes. Nothing about reading a deck word-for-word captivates the attendees, and your aim is to keep people interested in your presentation.

If you need to, work on your public speaking skills. Practice at home in front of a mirror, video yourself and watch it back, or practice with friends and family who can provide you with honest, constructive feedback. Then you must assume the responsibility to improve on your presentation style. Work on your tone, body language, eye contact, and of course the content (content is King!). If you are thorough and prepared, knowing well the content of your presentation, your confidence will follow. Presenting an unclear, incomplete, or disorganized pitch which leaves everyone saying, "Uhmm, okay..." will befuddle your audience. If you are engaging, organized and self-assured, you will keep people's attention and to them, you will be a plus.

When people are put to sleep by your monotone voice and statue-like posture, then you have lost them. Remember my note in Chapter 1 about the importance of eye contact? An acquaintance of mine once had a university professor who fixed his gaze on the wall at the back of the room in every class. Every single lecture. He never made eye contact with any of the thirty or so students in the room. A potentially interesting course left the students bored and mocking the professor because of his stiff and impersonal presentation style. Don't be remembered for that. Be remembered for your remarkable content and presentation style.

I once worked with someone who struggled to grasp the basic concept of Salesforce CRM and therefore couldn't properly show the work effort. As a result, that person was constantly lost at each meeting, and thus was unable to walk us through the work they had done. Imagine you're doing a presentation but are unable to keep track of what you are saying and often times find yourself saying, "Uhh, where was I? Uhh, let me find that." I did not blame the person in that situation; in my opinion, the company had failed to provide this individual with the basic training needed to adequately use a core tool to perform the role. I always wondered if management realized all those seconds this person was lost and confused was actually costing the company money. But at the same time, if you do find yourself in this position, take the initiative to ask for guidance ahead of time so that your presentation is well-polished.

If you don't believe there are downstream effects in a team when meetings standards remain subpar, consider this situation. I once gave myself the following excuse to not fully prepare for a team meeting: "Any effort will suffice for this

Chapter 3

management team, so why bother?" I thought. "Heck, if I come too prepared, the meeting might be too efficient. It could even finish early or on time. I mean, how would they handle a meeting with time not wasted?" When I presented, it was apparent how little prep time I had devoted in advance. I was disappointed in myself for making excuses to not perform at my best. At the next meeting, I redeemed myself and vowed to never again underperform for these reasons. That experience made me feel less than. I do not want to be a minus.

Remember, it doesn't matter why others don't live up to their abilities. You still have a responsibility to do your best, not so much for others but mainly for yourself. Sadly, the more suboptimal the environment, or in this case, the more an office accepts crummy performance within a team, the greater the impact over time, even on the most stellar members of the team.

To be frank, like many others such work environments have influenced my decision to leave companies in the past. The ripple effect is a very real thing!

Conclusion

Unless you are attending an information meeting as a passive observer and simply taking notes, your attendance likely comes with the expectation that you will add something to the meeting. I'll boldly claim that even at information meetings, chances are you may have a meaningful question to ask — one that no one else thought of and the answer to which may be useful for all in attendance. So ask. Bring more than yourself to the meeting — bring extra value with positive inputs. To the powers that be, remember to welcome comments from your junior colleagues as well.

In Bryant's article, Julie Greenwald, Chairwoman and COO of Atlantic Records is quoted as saying,

> In meetings, I constantly talk about how we have to be vulnerable, and that it's not fair for some people to just sit or stand along the wall and not participate. If you're not going to participate, then that means you're just sponging off the rest of us.[3]

While you may need to be a sponge to a certain extent to soak up information, also squeeze something out of yourself so that you're adding to the meeting, not just taking. If you're passing notes or chatting with the person beside you, if you're reading word-for-word from text-heavy slides when giving a presentation, or if you have no meaningful questions to ask and no answers to give when asked important questions, then you are a minus. Aim to leave the meeting capable of saying you spent the time being a plus.

Chapter 4

Invite the Right People

Ever been in a meeting where you were not only bored or confused but were asking yourself, "Why am I here?" Typically, moderators will invite all members of a team or even all staff members to a meeting, but not everyone necessarily needs to be present if the meeting doesn't apply to them.

As the moderator, ask yourself, "Do all these invitees need to be there?" If the honest answer is no, then don't invite certain people just for the sake of doing so.

Everyone likes to feel included, and people want to be in the know about what's happening, but as I mentioned in Chapter 2, people also don't want to feel like their time is being wasted. If you invite people to a meeting, they feel they are expected to attend and so they do, sometimes only to discover that there is nothing of value for them in the meeting, nor do they have anything to contribute. If that is the case, then they shouldn't be there.

Chapter 4

What's the Meeting Costing You?

No, I'm not talking about how much you spend on muffins and coffee.

Have you ever equated meeting time to people's salaries? At your next meeting, look around the room at who is there. How much does each person make per hour? And then ask yourself, "Is it worth the cost to the company for this person to be here?"

In Terri Williams's article, "How to stop wasting your time—and everyone else's— in meetings," Bonnie Hagemann, co-author of Leading with Vision describes calculating the cost of weekly executive meetings at a former workplace. Her math revealed that the weekly cost of those meetings was $10,000 based on the salaries of those who were in attendance.[1]

Are there information items that can be shared in an email or made available on a shared document which can be consulted anytime rather than being presented in a meeting? Why invite people to a meeting primarily to go over a slide presentation that you can just as easily email to everyone unless an in-person discussion of the content is vital? If the presentation is extensive and is for information only, email it and don't bother with the meeting.

Also, if there are attendees who would be expected to speak for two minutes or less, can they instead give their update on a shared document, thus allowing them to keep working, rather than attend the meeting yet still update the team? It serves the company no purpose to have them there for fifty-eight minutes when their presence at a meeting is only needed for two minutes. Their time instead could be devoted to making headway on their specific responsibilities. If you do wish to have them present, give them the opportunity to pop into the meeting for a few minutes to present their information but then release them from the rest of the meeting that doesn't apply to them.

According to Moira Alexander, "US businesses lose around $37 billion each year due to unnecessary meetings, and the time lost and opportunity cost due to unproductive meetings can be compounded if there are unnecessary attendees."[2] What's the cost of your weekly meetings? Are you getting enough bang for your buck? If not, streamline your attendee list.

Include the Right People

It may seem obvious that those who are directly involved in the project at hand should have a place at the meeting table, but depending on the purpose of the meeting and what the agenda items are, not everyone on the team may need to be there.

Alexander recommends the following when deciding who needs to attend a meeting:

Chapter 4

1. Consider the purpose of the meeting and invite only those who are needed based on the purpose of the meeting.

2. Identify those who have expertise on the subject of the meeting and can contribute by sharing their expertise.

3. Invite anyone who has pertinent updates to share.

4. Invite those who need to hear the updates.[3]

In addition, Tom LaForce, in his book *Meeting Hero*, recommends that you consider the following when determining who should be at a meeting:

1. Avoid the people you know will create problems.

2. Bring in the best people who are available.

3. Find people who can wear multiple hats.

4. Watch out for politics.

5. Consider some unlikely choices.[4]

You may be in a position where you have no choice but to include people who bring problems or politics with them or who detract from the focus. As discussed previously, it's the moderator's job to address this type of behavior.

From the above list, points number three and five are worth emphasizing. Your organization may be starting a new project and you're looking to put a team together, or perhaps you have a project that is underway but the momentum has stalled. Look around your organization. Chances are you have people on other teams or in other roles who have hidden and/or untapped talents. I'm not advocating for adding to someone's workload when they already have a full plate, but maybe you have someone in the organization who would be valuable to a particular project, and perhaps that person would be excited for a change or for a chance to contribute to something outside the scope of their normal work. If you have gaps on your team, survey your staff and see who can fill these holes. Someone might surprise you with an amazing contribution you may never have imagined.

For example, an acquaintance of mine worked as a high school teacher. She was hired as an English teacher and loved her role, but she had completed a double major in her degree: English Language Arts and Social Studies. For several years, she had casually mentioned to the principal that she would be interested in teaching Social Studies "someday." When a senior Social Studies teacher retired, the principal tapped this person on the shoulder. It just so happened she was ready for a change; the timing was perfect, and it was a win-win for both the school and the teacher. This person remained on staff, yet her expertise was still available to the English teachers even though she took on a different role.

If someone has talents that haven't been utilized, or if someone in the organization has changed roles, they will likely have something to offer to a team they aren't officially part of, and they could certainly be included in meetings when appropriate.

Conversely, if you invite people who don't need to be there, you are wasting their time. They may quickly realize this and, as often happens, do their own work on their laptop during the meeting. Wouldn't it be better for everyone if that person were back in their office doing work rather than taking up space in a meeting room, distracting from the meeting by clicking on their keyboard, and being in a situation where they are only partially attentive to both the meeting and the work they are doing?

Conclusion

Many people assume that because they've been invited to a meeting, therefore they must attend. It's true that no one wants to say no when asked to do something, especially when asked by a superior, and that includes being asked to attend meetings. But one way to free yourself from unnecessary meetings is to just say no to attending a meeting at which you know you will not be needed and cannot contribute. Ask yourself two questions:

1. Do I have something to contribute to the meeting?

2. Is there something for me to learn at this meeting?

If your answer to both questions is no, then you really don't need to attend the meeting and your manager will likely appreciate your saying so.

Chapter 5

Have Fewer Meetings

Assume you have to review and report on ten proposals or grant requests each week. But, imagine having two or three meetings a day at least three days of the week. How can you provide detailed enough updates on all of them at these meetings when you probably have not had time to fully evaluate them?

Yes, there can be such a thing as too many meetings. I worked at a place that conducted meetings three to five days a week, and at times there would be two or three meetings daily. It seemed to me that a lot of the information could have been communicated via email and worse, the meetings were happening prematurely. What really struck me many times was how often those meetings prevented others from actually doing work. As a result, most staff often talked about squeezing personal time around weekend work in order to catch up because they couldn't complete their tasks at the office given they were running from meetings to meetings.

Chapter 5

In one of those meetings, I finally spoke up and asked whether there were too many meetings and if management considered what impact all these meetings were having on everyone's ability to complete their work. The senior executives decided to experiment with meeting once every two weeks for the next two months to test whether staff would have more updates and make more headway on their files once there were fewer meetings. For the remainder of my time there, we met less and less frequently and got more and more work done.

Even when there are fewer meetings though, make sure they are still run effectively. As <u>Perlow</u> points out,

> Some organizations have relatively few meetings but run them poorly. As a result, individuals have sufficient time for solo tasks and deep thinking, but group productivity and collaboration are weakened because each meeting is inefficient.[1]

Add Meetings (But of Different Types)

Although adding meetings to your schedule may sound counterintuitive, Ben Johnson, in "<u>4 Ways to Have Fewer Meetings at Work</u>," recommends scheduling a "daily huddle" each morning for five to ten minutes to start the work day; this can result in less time spent in meetings overall. The huddle serves as a chance for all team members to briefly share and discuss daily updates with one another in the conference room, and when combined with "weekly all-hands" meetings that are limited to one hour, provide his team the opportunity to remain regularly and closely connected to one another as work progresses. He expounds that the weekly and daily touch points, totalling one and a half hours per week, have resulted in less time spent overall in meetings since team members are consistently up to date and well-connected with one another.[2]

And Then Subtract

Similarly, Samantha Stone, in "How to have fewer meetings" suggests scheduling "No Meeting" times in your schedule, just as you would schedule a meeting in your calendar, so that you can block off times for working productively. She recommends doing this not only individually but also as a corporation: "Many companies dedicate one day per week to pure work — so no meetings allowed."[3]

Stewart Butterfield, chief of Slack, goes one step further by recommending that you cancel all meetings and then take a look at which ones you actually miss. He suggests this extreme measure as a way to evaluate which meetings are truly needed and which are unnecessary: "We probably do need some of the ones we canceled, and they'll come back — but we'll wait until we actually need them again,"[4] he states in Bryant's article.

Use Collaboration Tools

In addition to the shift to virtual meetings, constantly evolving and varying technologies continue to offer increasing options that can replace formal meetings. Take advantage of these innovations and use them to streamline your work processes.

Given the surge in remote work, and with globalization requiring people to collaborate across time zones, it's not always possible to meet in real time. Email "meetings" allow for conversation across time zones and enable people to contribute to the discourse at their convenience. The added benefit of email exchanges is having a written record of the comments and points raised so that discussion can be reviewed later. In case of disagreement, the written record can be retrieved to clarify misunderstandings.

Corporate Wiki has become increasingly vital for collaboration. Google Docs, One Drive, and Dropbox are great options for sharing documents as alternatives to emailing documents. Additional tools like Slack, Trello and others provide ancillary collaborative options. As more and more people are working virtually, you can take advantage of these types of tools to replace real-time (whether it's in-person or virtual) meetings. Beth Carter, in her "12 Top Online Collaboration Tools for Virtual Teams" evaluates twelve such tools, outlining what she feels are the benefits and drawbacks of each.[5]

Conclusion

Face-to-face or virtual meetings are not the only options for collaborating and sharing. Traditional meetings, while not yet "a thing of the past," are not necessarily the only or even the best option for gathering people and working together. As time goes on, more options are presenting themselves, allowing for organizations to reduce and, in some cases, eliminate "The Meeting."

Time will tell if the face of workplace meetings will permanently change. So far, technology has certainly brought to light the wide variety of innovative options available — do use collaboration tools instead of holding meetings.

Chapter 6

Close the Loop

Gain Traction (Don't Spin Your Wheels)

Effective meetings serve to move the project and overall company goals farther by closing the loop back on pending questions from previous meetings and then looking at the next steps (more on "next steps" in Chapter 7).

Unlike many people, especially women, I am not afraid to speak up. Although I am naturally reserved, long ago, I made the decision to never be shy about asking for clarification at my job to ensure that I understand my responsibilities and expectations. Yet, I hesitate to talk in meetings because as a junior employee, it can feel as if I'm taking up space. I tend to adhere to an unspoken rule that the purpose of my presence is mainly to listen but not to take up too much time during meetings. (All bench players understand their role. Do you want to hear from Lebron or What's-his-face/Whatchamacallum?) I can't even imagine what it must feel like for a less confident individual who may have a meaningful contribution to

Chapter 6

make but is afraid to speak up. When I ask a question during a meeting, I do so based on the judgement that the answer will be to every attendees' gain, not just my own.

Now, consider when a junior associate works up the courage to ask a question but gets told the answer will be provided at the next meeting. However, at the next meeting, if the answer is still not provided, then it means that staff member must wrestle with the option of taking up space once again only to raise that same question. Otherwise, some aspect of this person's tasks will stall. In other words, an answer is instrumental for that employee to close the loop on important items.

Having faced a similar situation, I was left debating whether people thought that I detracted from important objectives or used too much time given my tiny part in the big picture of the meeting and more so the company. But an answer to my question was crucial to my job performance as well as moving project goals forward. Therefore, I needed to ask it again even though I would have preferred to not put myself on the spot twice, which could have been avoided if there had been emphasis on closing the loop.

A friend who works at a New Age/New Thought firm said their meetings have become a full hourlong show focused on the personal life of the CEO. So every Monday morning, staff shows up to these inescapable meetings, which no longer serve their purpose of pushing company objectives forward.

Perlow points out that leaving next steps unclear results in more time being wasted in sidebar conversations after the meeting because staff want to confirm the action plans.[1]

What is the purpose of the meeting if not to clarify those next steps? If your agenda doesn't include an action plan, or if the action plan isn't clear to all attendees by the time they leave, then the meeting did not fully achieve its purpose. Thus, it bears reiterating, be sure that the loop has been closed on agenda items before everyone leaves the meeting.

Conclusion

Team members need to feel empowered. The most productive workers are those who take pride in their work and enjoy what they are doing. Confusion, lack of direction, and gaping holes in communication only serve to waste more time and diminish people's confidence. Aim to end meetings having tied up any loose threads and knowing who is doing what — and why. Send team members forth from the meeting room feeling that they are valued members of a well-oiled machine. Make certain that they leave the meeting feeling confident, determined, and motivated to do their part to move that machine onwards.

More on this in the final chapter.

Chapter 7

Build on the Overall Goal

Set the Tone Again

In one group project that I was part of, every time that the team met, we talked about key deliverables needed in order to advance the project. Unfortunately, whenever we met for a status update, most people would simply discuss their inability to complete their assigned work. Even worse, most of the team members would come to meeting after meeting and say that they hadn't done anything but offer no reason other than that they had not prioritized the project. All too often, their update was, "There is nothing to update," and so there was no point to the meeting!

What stayed with me was how the leader of the working group never took measures to rectify this issue. Obviously those members were not performing, yet the leader neglected to take corrective measures. Needless to say, not only did the project never move ahead, but we had a steady stream of unnecessary meetings where all that was accomplished was reaffirming that nothing had been done.

Chapter 6

At a different workplace, an external firm would facilitate well-structured meetings in support of business development and overall sales strategies. Sounds great right? Except the leader of the company displayed no commitment to whatever plans and goals derived from these meetings. As a matter of fact, it always seemed like information went in one ear and out the other. At that company, nearly everyone had a downtrodden attitude. Since the leader showed clear indifference to growth objectives after every meeting, that attitude was also reflected by many of the employees. It is very hard to keep people enthused within a team when the leader doesn't portray an optimistic, productive attitude. In retrospect, this may have to do with lack of discipline and vision on the part of this CEO, but the result was a general languid mood inside the organization. There was a lack of concern and enthusiasm for growth, likewise, the absence of that sense/pride employees feel, thus assume a vested interest in companywide success.

As a junior person, when you witness the leader taking a passive or dismissive attitude towards a project, it's hard to take it seriously yourself. As I covered in Chapter 1, and as Bryant emphasizes, "When establishing the informal rules of an organization, employees take their cues from the person in the corner office."[1] The leader/moderator sets the tone for the meeting, for the project, and for the organization.

As the leader on a project, it is your responsibility to make sure that deliverables are moving along, and you are also tasked with calling and executing purposeful meetings. If nothing has been done — if there is nothing to report — there is no need to meet. Instead of holding the scheduled meeting, touch base with team members one-on-one to ensure they are working on their individual tasks and then when necessary, call the group together for productive meetings that will help keep the project moving forward.

If the project is not progressing, it is the leader's responsibility to kickstart the process again. Leaders, you may need to put a little pressure on people to maintain the momentum. Make it clear that ABC needs to be completed by the next meeting, and then set the next meeting as the checkpoint for reviewing ABC and then moving on to DEF.

Decide Who Carries the Ball

A final emphasis on and a reminder of the tasks and goals to be completed before the next meeting will leave team members with the one thought in their minds: I need to do "this" by "then."

One of my former colleagues, who now works at a higher learning institution, shared that most poorly run meetings she attended lacked structure and a clear agenda, which led to attendees speaking tangentially as well as there being no clear action items/objectives to take away post meeting.

Chapter 6

<u>Bryant</u> presents a great sports metaphor, as explained by Shellye Archambeau, Chief Executive of MetricStream, who, at the end of each meeting, asks, "Who's got the ball?" In soccer, football, baseball, tennis, etc., whoever has the ball is responsible for what happens next, and so Archambeau suggests ending each meeting by clarifying who has "the ball" and what they will be doing with it before the next meeting. Specifying who has the ball makes that person accountable. All team members know who is holding the ball and expect that person or those people to report at the next meeting on the action they accepted (the ball).[2]

In order to keep projects moving and team members accountable, reiterate and emphasize your action plan at the end of the meeting. Do a quick wrap up to discuss next steps. Review who is responsible for what items, and restate deadlines for any actions that are to be taken.

In short, end each meeting with an emphasis on the following:

- Who is "doing?"
- What are they doing?
- When will it be completed?

Conclusion

As a meeting attendee, your responsibility is to leave meetings well-informed and equipped to better perform your role of helping the company achieve its desired results.

As a leader or moderator, it is your responsibility to schedule and plan for meetings that will support employees and attendees in fulfilling their responsibilities. At the conclusion of meetings, send your team members forth knowing what the action plans are, understanding who is responsible for what, and feeling inspired to do their part to help achieve the company's goals.

Afterword

If your meetings aren't as productive and effective as they can be, take some time to evaluate the reasons for the inefficiencies. As Perlow emphasizes, it is "critical to regularly and openly take stock of how people feel about the meetings they attend and about their work process more generally."[1] You can then use that feedback and implement the ideas in this book to right your ship.

Meetings can and should be enjoyable (whether you have delicious snacks or not) and worthwhile. Meetings are necessary in order to dispense information, discuss updates, make decisions, solve problems, build corporate culture, and determine action plans for moving projects onward. But what's more important than having the meeting is having useful meetings.

This book is my call to other junior staff that, although you are less accountable than senior management, you owe it to colleagues to bring your A game; feel compelled to be a plus on the team. It is also my tap on the shoulder to leaders, moderators who need to streamline and hold more effective meetings.

Acknowledgments

I've wanted to write this book for a few years...there's never a great time to do something. You simply have to do it!

We've all heard the saying, "It takes a village to raise a child." Well, in my case, it took many people, most to remain unnamed, who contributed to this body of work. Particularly, I thank these subsequent individuals whose invaluable contribution aided tremendously in accomplishing this milestone.

My family and friends for support and encouragement. Specifically, with a more hands-on contribution is my sister, Shiva K. Peter. Her exquisite design skills were handy in developing the cover and other aesthetics.

I first began having deep, dare I say, philosophical discussions about effective meetings with an acquaintance trained in philosophy, Dr. Jean-Jacques Rousseau. The time spent under his tutelage, devoted towards fine-tuning my intellectual development, helped influence the content of this publication and shaped me into a much more logical person.

The next person I've held sound and concrete talks with about this topic is John E. Cushnie. He also lent his skills as an editor as well as provided

Acknowledgments

valuable feedback, which made this an even better piece of art.

Lastly, I am truly beholden to my former professor, Madame Danica Lavoie. Her work as the final editor was indispensable. The corrections, insights, and advice she provided were *nonpareil*[1] and reflect her support for, commitment to, and trust in her students.

Even with a great team and support, I am solely responsible and accountable for the contents of this book.

From me to you: My inaugural *pièce de resistance*

.

About the Author

Nava Laguerre has multidisciplinary interests and is passionate about continuous learning and growth. One of her many interests is the timely and well-disciplined execution of meetings.

Nava lives in Canada surrounded by her many books.

References

Alexander, Moira. "6 quick ways to decide who to invite to a project meeting." TechRepublic. December 1, 2017. Accessed March 6th, 2021 from https://www.techrepublic.com/article/6-quick-ways-to-decide-who-should-be-invited-to-a-project-meeting/

Bryant, Adam. "How to Run a More Effective Meeting." The New York Times Business. Accessed March 13, 2021 from https://www.nytimes.com/guides/business/how-to-run-an-effective-meeting

Carter, Beth. "12 Top Online Collaboration Tools for Virtual Teams." March 31, 2017. Clariant Creative. Accessed March 6, 2021 from https://www.clariantcreative.com/blog/online-collaboration-tools-for-virtual-team

Frisch, Bob and Cary Greene. "Make Time for Small Talk in your Virtual Meetings." Harvard Business Review. February 18, 2021. Accessed March 14, 2021 from https://hbr.org/2021/02/make-time-for-small-talk-in-your-virtual-meetings

Indeed Career Guide. "How to Write a Meeting Agenda: Tips, Template and Sample." November 25, 2020 accessed March 5th from https://www.indeed.com/career-advice/career-development/how-to-write-a-meeting-agenda

Johnson, Ben. "4 Ways to Have Fewer Meetings at Work." Zapier. November 25, 2019. Accessed March 6, 2021 from https://zapier.com/blog/reduce-meetings/

LaForce, Tom. "Invite the Right People to your Meeting." Meeting Hero (book) Accessed March 5, 2021 from https://themeetinghero.com/invite-the-right-people-to-your-meeting/

Maxwell, John C. "Are You a Plus or a Minus?" YouTube video, 1:37, May 13, 2019, Accessed March 13, 2021 from https://www.youtube.com/watch?v=2efYkADfHrE

MeetingSift. "The Six Most Common Types of Meetings." Accessed March 3, 2021 from http://meetingsift.com/the-six-types-of-meetings/

Mueller, Annie. "The Cost of Hiring a New Employee." Investopedia. Updated June 16, 2020. Accessed March 26, 2021 from https://www.investopedia.com/financial-edge/0711/the-cost-of-hiring-a-new-employee.aspx

Perlow, Leslie. "Stop the Meeting Madness." Harvard Business Review. July-August 2017. Accessed March 6, 2021 from https://hbr.org/2017/07/stop-the-meeting-madness

Potter, Jamie. "Why Do Employees Hate Meetings, And What Can Be Done To Make Them Better?" February 8, 2020. Accessed March 5, 2021 from https://www.forbes.com/sites/jaimepotter/2020/02/08/why-do-employees-hate-meetings-and-what-can-be-done-to-make-them-better/?sh=5013794d874b

Stone, Samantha. "How to have fewer meetings." April 6, 2020. Accessed March 6th, 2021 from https://medium.com/@samantha.stone/how-to-have-fewer-meetings-26fbad8a28ed

Williams, Terri. "How to stop wasting time—yours and everyone else's—at meetings." Accessed March 4, 2021 from https://execed.economist.com/blog/industry-trends/how-stop-wasting-your-time-and-everyone-elses-meetings

1 Leslie Perlow. "Stop the Meeting Madness." Harvard Business Review. July-August 2017. Accessed March 6, 2021 from https://hbr.org/2017/07/stop-the-meeting-madness
2 Jamie Potter. "Why Do Employees Hate Meetings, And What Can Be Done To Make Them Better?" February 8, 2020. Accessed March 5, 2021 from https://www.forbes.com/sites/jaimepotter/2020/02/08/why-do-employees-hate-meetings-and-what-can-be-done-to-make-them-better/?sh=5013794d874b
1 Perlow. "Stop the Meeting Madness"
2 MeetingSift. "The Six Most Common Types of Meetings." Accessed March 3, 2021 from http://meetingsift.com/the-six-types-of-meetings/
3 *malsain*: unhealthy
4 *equipe*: team, small group
1 Adam Bryant. "How to Run a More Effective Meeting." The New York Times Business. Accessed March 13, 2021 from https://www.nytimes.com/guides/business/how-to-run-an-effective-meeting
2 Indeed Career Guide. "How to Write a Meeting Agenda: Tips, Template and Sample" November 25, 2020 accessed March 5th from https://www.indeed.com/career-advice/career-development/how-to-write-a-meeting-agenda
3 Terri Williams. "How to stop wasting time—yours and everyone else's—at meetings." Accessed March 4, 2021 from https://execed.economist.com/blog/industry-trends/how-stop-wasting-your-time-and-everyone-elses-meetings
4 *en passant*: by the way
5 Potter. "Why Do Employees Hate Meetings, And What Can Be Done To Make Them Better?"
6 Potter. "Why Do Employees Hate Meetings, And What Can Be Done To Make Them Better?"
7 Potter. "Why Do Employees Hate Meetings, And What Can Be Done To Make Them Better?"
8 Williams. "How to stop wasting time—yours and everyone else's—at meetings."
9 Bob Frisch and Cary Greene. "Make Time for Small Talk in your Virtual Meetings." Harvard Business Review. February 18, 2021. Accessed March 14, 2021 from https://hbr.org/2021/02/make-time-for-small-talk-in-your-virtual-meetings
10 Frisch and Greene. "Make Time for Small Talk in your Virtual Meetings."

1 John C. Maxwell. "Are You a Plus or a Minus?" YouTube video, 1:37, May 13, 2019, Accessed March 13, 2021 from https://www.youtube.com/watch?v=2efYkADfHrE
2 Bryant. "How to Run a More Effective Meeting."
3 Bryant. "How to Run a More Effective Meeting."
1 Williams. "How to stop wasting time—yours and everyone else's—at meetings."
2 Moira Alexander. "6 quick ways to decide who to invite to a project meeting." TechRepublic. December 1, 2017. Accessed March 6th, 2021 from https://www.techrepublic.com/article/6-quick-ways-to-decide-who-should-be-invited-to-a-project-meeting/
3 Alexander. "6 quick ways to decide who to invite to a project meeting."
4 Tom LaForce. "Invite the Right People to your Meeting." Meeting Hero (book) Accessed March 5, 2021 from https://themeetinghero.com/invite-the-right-people-to-your-meeting/
1 Perlow. "Stop the Meeting Madness"
2 Ben Johnson. "4 Ways to Have Fewer Meetings at Work." Zapier. November 25, 2019. Accessed March 6, 2021 from https://zapier.com/blog/reduce-meetings/
3 Samantha Stone. "How to have fewer meetings." April 6, 2020. Accessed March 6th, 2021 from https://medium.com/@samantha.stone/how-to-have-fewer-meetings-26fbad8a28ed
4 Bryant. "How to Run a More Effective Meeting."
5 Beth Carter. "12 Top Online Collaboration Tools for Virtual Teams." March 31, 2017. Clariant Creative. Accessed March 6, 2021 from https://www.clariantcreative.com/blog/online-collaboration-tools-for-virtual-team
1 Perlow. "Stop the Meeting Madness"
1 Bryant. "6 quick ways to decide who to invite to a project meeting."
2 Bryant. "How to Run a More Effective Meeting."
1 Perlow "Stop the Meeting Madness"
1 *Nonpareil*: unequaled, unrivaled

CPSIA information can be obtained
at www.ICGtesting.com
Printed in the USA
LVHW081330210721
693209LV00008B/387